IMAGES
of America

RED BANK

IMAGES
of America

RED BANK

Randall Gabrielan

ARCADIA

First published 1995
Copyright © Randall Gabrielan, 1995

ISBN 0-7524-0216-1

Published by Arcadia Publishing,
an imprint of the Chalford Publishing Corporation
One Washington Center, Dover, New Hampshire 03820
Printed in Great Britain

Library of Congress Cataloging-in-Publication Data applied for

To my dear wife Barbara Ann,
not only for her love, patience, and support,
but for facing the final frenzy in preparing this work in silent,
understanding forbearance. Barbara, I hope your second book in as
many years justifies the sometimes skewed priorities.

Contents

Acknowledgments

A special thanks to John Rhody, Robert Schoeffling, and Michael Steinhorn, who gave strong impetus to this project by opening their collections at the outset with an offer of whatever was needed. Bob Schoeffling's spirit merits special note: if he lacks what I need, he regrets it as much for the inability to help as for the gap in his collection.

Singular thanks to the Red Bank Public Library whose large photographic holdings, begun in 1937 by the donation of Howard Whitfield's collection, have new access via a 1994 preservation project which produced copy negatives and microfilm. This work is the first public use of the new forms in that rich collection.

The contributions of Photography Unlimited by Dorn's to photographing Red Bank have been mentioned in the text and deserve a second word here. They are the unofficial town photographic archives. Their holdings contributed significantly.

The Monmouth County Historical Association distinguishes itself in so many areas of collecting and preserving Monmouth County history. They have the distinction of having the oldest image in this book. I am deeply thankful for it and their other contributions.

The lenders of the photographs are the co-producers of this volume. My thanks and appreciation to each one. I am grateful that nearly all showed support and interest for the project extending beyond their picture loans, whether they numbered a single photograph or many. In addition to the above, they are: Edwin F. Banfield, Olga Boeckel, Mo Cuocci, Richard F. Doughty, Alex Finch, Les Horner, Gail Hunton, Catherine Ann Jacoby, Robert and Mary Johnson, Peggy Jordan, J. Louise Jost and the Shrewsbury Historical Society, W. Edmund Kemble, Evelyn Leavens, Kathleen McGrath, Timothy J. McMahon, Donald L. Magee, Susanna P. Maguire, John Mattocia, June Methot, George H. Moss Jr., the late John M. Pillsbury, Ralph A. Romeo, Karen L. Schnitzspahn, Grace Tetley, Keith Wells, Cynthia Wessel, and Lawrence E. White.

Red Bank: A Glimpse Into Its Past

A brief history of an old and active town is a daunting task. One begins well by referring the reader to the only full length work on the subject, Helen C. Phillips' *Red Bank on the Navesink*, and a second that covers the waterfront in depth, June Methot's *Up and Down the River*. In addition, the reader may consult the extensive Red Bank listing in Robert Van Benthuysen's 1974 *Monmouth County Bibliography*.

The picture captions help convey the history, but the inclusion of any site was subject to availability and the need to edit the large pictorial resources of an often-photographed town. Thus, churches, schools, and the major business thoroughfares are better represented than other sites and streets.

Red Bank, long part of Shrewsbury Township, one of Monmouth County's three original townships, is believed to have been first used as a locality name in 1736, when Thomas Morford sold Joseph French a lot of over 3 acres on the west side of the highway that goes to the red bank. Information on Red Bank's early settlement is sparse. Its modern history generally begins *c.* 1800 with Barnes Smock's purchase of a tract bordering the Navesink River. He opened a tavern, the all-purpose public building of its day, near the river, *c.* 1809.

The entries of the two great historical-descriptive works of the first half of the nineteenth century are inconsistent in their mention of Red Bank, but merit mention. Thomas F. Gorden's *A Gazeteer of the State of New Jersey* indicated that Red Bank "contains within a circle of a mile in diameter about 100 dwellings, 3 taverns and 4 stores." He mentioned that a steamboat was running to New York, that vacationing New Yorkers boarded with farmers, and that the river had been recently bridged. Barber and Howes' 1845 *Historical Collections of the State of New Jersey*, perhaps referring to a smaller town center, claimed that in 1830 Red Bank contained only two houses, including the tavern by the river, but by 1844 it contained seven stores, one hat manufacturer, two wheelwrights, two lumber yards, two blacksmiths, two lime kilns, one sash and and blind factory, a public meeting hall, an Episcopal church, and sixty dwellings. The town's principal commerce was New York City trade, with thirteen sloops and schooners and one steamboat on that route.

The time was opportune for growth in the New York maritime trade as the route was shortened by the 1830 opening of an inlet at Sandy Hook, which remained open to about 1848. Red Bank's expansion was even more dramatic in the 1860s after the arrival of the Raritan and Delaware Bay Railroad, a line later absorbed by the Central Railroad of New Jersey. The 1875 opening of the New York and Long Branch Railroad, the so-called "all land route," increased rail travel and traffic opportunities

Red Bank's first business district centered on the Front Street-Wharf Avenue corner, while the earliest residential neighborhoods developed in the Washington-Spring Street area. Mercantile and residential sections rose on Broad Street, a thoroughfare whose transition can be studied as a microcosm of the town's history. Front Street is a second combined commercial-residential street, with its early residences built on small lots near the town center. Larger waterfront estates were centered on Front's eastern stem, now known as River Road, an area that was sub-divided, primarily in the 1920s.

Red Bank was organized as a town within Shrewsbury Township in 1870. The tie remained close, with Shrewsbury Township building its municipal building on Monmouth Street in 1892. Total separation as a borough was attained in 1908. Red Bank's borders were initially smaller than they are today, but have been expanded several times.

The railroad helped spark Red Bank's participation in the late-nineteenth-century industrial boom. Several needle trades manufacturers located here, including what became a massive uniform factory owned by Sigmund Eisner. The railroad tended to separate the town, with business focused on the west side and residential communities on the east side.

The railroad also aided Red Bank's emergence as a shopping town. Initially, it served the agricultural population of the surrounding towns, and later (and still) a growing suburban population. That role was altered forever with the 1959 opening of the Monmouth Shopping Center, now Mall, in Eatontown. The latest of several efforts to revitalize the business district is, at the time of this writing, providing new vigor to downtown, assisted by shoppers rediscovering the appeal of street shopping.

Red Bank, as a large sectional commercial town, was the center of the region's photographers. Three notables left a sizable body of work on the townscape and its populace: Charles Foxwell (see p. 112), Joseph Dickopf, and Andrew Coleman (see p. 113) are standouts from the turn of the century and later. The first two competed in the burgeoning postcard trade in the ten years or so from 1903. Foxwell's street scenes are a particularly rich source for pictorial documentation of the major business streets. He also photographed numerous private residences. These pictures, if collected, would provide great architectural insight into a major period of Red Bank's housing growth.

Dorn is a Red Bank photographic family in its third generation. Daniel du B. Dorn (1883–1956) moved to Red Bank in 1916. His credits include early filmmaking, both for Fox Movietone News and his own production company. He was an inventor and created some of his photographic equipment. His son, Daniel Whitfield Dorn, founded the Dorn's Photo Shop in 1937, became a pilot, and flew as an aerial photographer during World War II, later photographing Monmouth County from the air. The third generation includes Daniel W.'s son, also a Daniel, a daughter, Kathy Dorn Severini, and a nephew, James. One branch of the family business, Photography Unlimited by Dorn's, includes a large archive of historical prints, a collection that is still expanding. Many of its fine images are illustrated herein, not only those marked "The Dorn's Collection," but others unlabeled that have been contributed by their owners, as the collection has long been accessible to the public by purchase.

Omissions of worthy subjects stem from a lack of photographs and/or space constraints. Red Bank's rich photographic resources can readily fill a second volume—indeed, a volume two is planned. The author is grateful to the lenders for this work, and seeks additional pictures for the next book; he may be reached at 71 Fish Hawk Drive, Middletown, New Jersey 07748, or at (908) 671 2645.

One
Broad Street

Benjamin W. Spinning bought the Isaac P. White store at the southwest corner of Broad and Front Streets, forming a partnership with Thomas Morford, which lasted until 1872. Thus, there is a seven-year time frame for this unsigned, gray painting, which was probably commissioned to reflect pride of ownership and, perhaps, to advertise the business. It is the oldest image in the book. See the bottom of p. 10 for the building there now. (Collection of the Monmouth County Historical Association.)

The west side of Broad Street south from Front as it appeared in New York's *The Daily Graphic* of July 26, 1878. The spire denotes the First Methodist Church, while the First National Bank is obscured behind it to the south. The largest of the stores past the corner is the J.H. Peters Co., which enjoyed the reputation as the finest housewares and dry goods emporium in the area. They all burned in the fire of November 5, 1882 . . .

. . . which started in Child's barn, behind their bakery a few doors from the corner. The brick Spinning and Patterson Building, which replaced the structure on p. 9, was saved through the great exertions of its occupants who kept moist cloth draped over the edge of the roof. Child's horses were saved, but the fire spread to the store, and to the others on both sides of it, including J.R. Bergen's brick shoe store. The *Register*, on the third floor, issued an extra edition the next day containing a lengthy account of the fire.

The library's photograph is labeled "1879 fire." It may picture the aftermath of the New Year's Eve fire that began in Jacob Naftal's menswear store. Inadequate water and fire-fighting equipment permitted the fire to get out of control and it eventually destroyed much of the east side of the Broad Street business district. A frame building was torn down to halt the fire's spread. Four serious fires in two years brought water supply to the fore as the key public issue of the day. (Collection of the Red Bank Public Library.)

This often reproduced c. 1880 view north on Broad Street did not result in a sign ordinance. Mrs. Alice Ludlow, whose Temple of Fashion is at the right, was arguably the leading clothier of her day, while Professor Allstron was the town's most highly regarded musician. So show some restraint in the signage. Compare the former's with the restrained Clayton and Magee's streamline-lettered, baked enamel sign, itself a modern classic. The fancy, pressed-metal cornices next to Ludlow are gone, with this illustration, perhaps, providing a restoration model.

Charles Foxwell's *c.* 1905 photograph of Broad Street looking south from Front is from the same perspective as the pre-fire view on p. 10. The building below can be seen in its street context. The Child Building to its right was damaged by fire in 1917. Its pedimented cornice elaboration is gone.

After the 1882 fire, James Peters replaced the town's fanciest store with its tallest building, as illustrated at left. The Peters Building was bought after his death by Robert Hance and his sons and renamed the Hance Building. The Broad Street National Bank was organized in 1919 and began operations on Monmouth Street. They acquired the Hance Building in 1920 and made extensive alterations designed by Perth Amboy architect J. Noble Pierson. The later remodeling had a streamlined look, embracing the round arch present in so many of the late-nineteenth-century Commercial Italianate buildings, and one still remains despite the marring of the building by openings at street level. The "BSNB" crest is still over the fifth story. The pictures came from the bank's condensed financial statements of 1929 and 1932.

The view south a block from Front places the east side's present and former stand-out buildings in their street perspective. The pedimented cornice in the foreground is the Temple of Fashion, while the tower in the background is the Second National Bank Building. The business district was still only about two and one-half blocks long *c.* 1910.

Bried's Cheap Cash Market was on the east side of Broad Street, between Mechanic and Wallace. It makes one nostalgic for a time when credit charges were not contemplated in retail pricing. Red Bank's 1903 fire district ordinance forbade the construction of frame buildings in the business district. Note Sloat's Undertaking, which also did upholstery. The building to the far right is #38, helping to date the picture prior to the *c.* 1900 renumbering of Broad Street, when odd numbers were assigned on the east side. (The Dorn's Collection.)

The five, small, one-story stores at the foot of Broad have survived threats to their existence that must date a century or more. They arose anew whenever extending Broad Street to the river was suggested. As John W. Stout was building near the site in 1881, a *Register* reporter heard his response when his opinion was sought on the proposed extension: "Well, I offered the property to the town once for $200. a foot front, but they'll never get such a chance again" (November 16, 1881).

Reconstruction after the 1880s fires helped create Broad Street's cohesive appearance, one strained over the years by "modernized" store fronts and threatened by extensive remodeling. One hopes the vintage photos will provide restoration inspiration over the next generation, so that the following generation will wonder how numbers 7 and 15 could have been so altered *c.* 1980.

Broad Street looking north from the middle of the block between Monmouth and White Streets, *c.* 1910. The information on the *Register* sign helps in dating pictures. The outlines of its last painting were visible until July 1995, when a yellow covering may have obliterated it forever. The Cooper Drug Store is underneath the sign. The building still stands, with its upper story removed. Today, the stores on the left are unrecognizable due to extensive remodeling.

The Broad Street block between Front and Mechanic (east), and White Street (west), was largely built-up by 1910. White was a model of restraint in advertising shoes. On p. 14, they were merely billed as "good." Here, they "wear."

R. Taylor Smock's dry goods business in the Esek White store on the northeast corner of Broad and Mechanic Streets was sold to A. Salz & Co., a Keyport firm. Joseph Salz managed the store and bought the growing business in 1896, erecting in 1903 the then modern building at the right of the opposite picture. This one is *c.* 1880s.

The corner of Broad and Mechanic in the early twentieth century with the Salz Building at left and the Wild Building at right. The *Saturday Evening Post* being sold by the boys has its cover picture readily discernable, which could aid a precise dating of the picture. (The Dorn's Collection.)

16

Despite the obscured view of the Salz store (at right), it should still convey that Red Bank retail architecture had entered a new era. The large windows provided light on an unprecedented scale. Joseph Swanell was the architect. The front has been redesigned and the entrance moved closer to Mechanic Street. The fire truck is returning to Navesink Hook & Ladder just down the street. (The Dorn's Collection.)

The 1874 H.N. Wild Building, its builder and construction readily marked by a date stone on the facade, is an early, substantial expression of a landlord's confidence in the business future of the town. Horatio Wild was a wealthy New York candy merchant and built this as an investment, intended for multiple tenants.

The carriages of a prior generation provided transportation for activities such as this pleased group's Broad Street outing in 1930.

This view is not much earlier than the February 1916 postmark on the card. The age of the automobile was beginning, as evidenced by the directional instructions on the old fountain. Note the early parallel parking, which would be replaced for decades by angle parking. A second clock was on the west side, near the Front Street corner.

The Neoclassical bank building at 53 Broad Street, at its northeast corner with Wallace Street, was designed by New York architect Warrington G. Lawrence for the First National Bank. However, the new building was occupied by the Red Bank Trust company. They absorbed First National in May 1914 just as the building was completed. Red Bank Trust merged with Second National Bank. The combined organization called themselves the name reflected in this c. 1920s picture, the Second National Bank and Trust Co.

The Presbyterian Church in Red Bank was organized in June 1852. Their church on the northeast corner of Broad and Wallace Streets was well south of the short business district when built. It was in use until 1911 when it was sold for the construction of the bank building there now, pictured on the opposite page. This postcard view was taken a few years before its demolition.

This view of Broad, looking north from White Street, shows how Peters' five-story building rose over its neighbors. The Cooper Pharmacy (below) is in the corner building at the left. The sidewalk canopies persist on the east side, providing some respite from the afternoon sun in an era well before air conditioning.

James Cooper's pharmacy in the Broadmeadow Building at the northwest corner of Broad and White Streets stands out in streetscapes due to its locale under the familiar *Register* sign painted on its building to the north. Cooper bought the Samuel Lockwood drug business there in 1881, forming a partnership with Riviere H. Sneden, buying the latter's interest after his death. Cooper packaged his own line of drugs under the name of "Aunt Mary's" remedies, doing quite well with cough medicine. The store contained a soda fountain and a station of the Tabard Inn library. (From the June 1904 *Industrial Recorder*.)

Isaac Adlem and Christopher Cole founded their dry goods business in 1863. Their 1868 purchase of Captain Christopher Doughty's house for a business building was considered foolhardy as this site, which became 30 Broad Street, was outside the short Broad Street business district. The Italianate arch, Broad Street's predominate design motif, is handsomely expressed in the original storefront. The photograph is likely *c.* 1880. It shows the corner of the Chadwick residence at left and the First National Bank at right. The latter was built in 1864 and destroyed in the fire of 1882. (Collection of the Red Bank Public Library.)

Cole retired in 1900, selling his interest to George Sutton, with the firm continuing as Adlem & Co. They remodeled the front in 1913, eliminating a staircase to the second floor, while increasing window space. The metal cornice replicates that of their now business neighbor on the south. At the right is the corner of the 1927 Merchants Trust Company Building. Adlem & Co. sold to Jacob Yanko in 1921. who had conducted a Red Bank store for eight years and another in New York for twelve years prior to that. The picture is likely *c.* 1930. (Collection of the Monmouth County Historical Association.)

Arthur F. Swift bought the Dr. Charles Hubbard lot on the northwest corner of Broad and Monmouth Streets and built the three-story building and office at the left, designed by Robert D. Chandler. The Patterson stores built in 1905 are the two-story buildings beyond it. The site around Moody's sign marks the area of the Eisner office, built in 1911, giving a six-year bracket for dating this photograph. (Collection of Michael Steinhorn.)

North of White Street was long known as the Haddon block as the stores were built on the site of William Haddon's home. The remodeled buildings still stand. The fence at the left marks John Sutton's house lot where the Eisner office was built. Photographer Joseph Dickopf claimed to be the first to combine a photography studio with an art shop. (The Dorn's Collection.)

Moody secured a shop at 48 Broad Street in time to appear in the June 1904 *Industrial Recorder* with this photograph. He carried a full line of leather goods. Note the call bell and the display of stock, including the coiled whip.

HARNESS.

We continue in the lead for all kinds of good custom made harness. We also handle all grades of factory made harness, trunks, bags and suit cases, gloves and mittens, dog collars, etc. In fact, everything that goes to make up a first-class harness store.

Our motto : Good goods at low prices. Note the name and number.

George Moody, born 1858 in Bradford County, Pennsylvania, opened a harness shop on west Front Street in 1896. He was a self-made success, starting his business with little capital, securing his first stock on credit. (From the *Register* of November 5, 1902.)

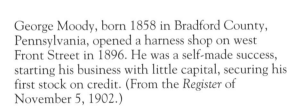

MOODY'S HARNESS STORE,
33 to 35 W. Front St., Red Bank.
GEORGE A. MOODY, Manager.

23

The George Hance Patterson stores, now the Rocar Building at 60 Broad Street, were designed by Fred Truex and built in 1905. Patterson purchased his deceased father-in-law Robert Allen's house and moved it around the corner to clear the site for Broad Street's advancing business district. Henry A. Guyon was a New York violinist who bought the Red Bank piano business of Curtis, Davis, and Hill in 1900. Mathushek remained on Broad Street until being purchased by the Tusting Piano Company, the county's oldest, in 1916.

Leon de la Reussille, a native of Bern, Switzerland, opened a Broad Street jewelry store in 1886, moving to the Blumenberg Building in 1902. He had earlier worked in his brother Alphonses' shop in Freehold, the family having been clock and watch makers for generations. Reusille held the position of inspector of watches for the Central Railroad of New Jersey. The landmark lollipop clock was installed shortly after the relocation. This view, with carnival bunting, is c. 1905. (The Dorn's Collection.)

A *c.* 1905 Foxwell view of the west side of Broad Street south of White Street. The two buildings to the right of the Sugar Bowl sign were destroyed by fire in 1978. The First National Bank behind the sign was by then built out to the street's building line. DeHart & Letson, another photographer active then, can be seen on the right. They were better known for their portraits, although some streetscapes are known. J. Kridel had four Red Bank locations before buying the Spinning and Patterson Building at the corner of Front in 1914, which they occupied as a menswear store until selling the business in 1946 to the Natelson brothers.

The July 4, 1946 parade honoring World War II veterans attracted what was called the largest crowd ever to gather in Red Bank, an estimated 15,000. An even larger number attended a fireworks display that night. An honor detachment was made-up of 300 veterans. The 2.5-mile parade is shown proceeding south on Broad Street on its way to the Red Bank athletic field. The Red Bank VFW post won the trophy for the best float.

The three-story building at the southeast corner of Broad and Wallace Streets was built for the Mercantile Bank, *c.* 1898. It was regarded then as the town's finest commercial structure. The property was bought by the Second National Bank and occupied by them in 1905. The post office was in one of the building's stores.

The Second National merged with the Red Bank Trust Co. *c.* 1924. They occupied the building on the opposite corner (see p. 19) and the banking premises in the building at top was remodeled for stores. It appears that subsequent remodeling removed the offices for reasons not clear, but they may have involved the elimination of internal support as the first-floor space was opened. Sun Ray Drugs occupied the place in the 1940s. (The Dorn's Collection.)

This picture is labeled in the collection of the Red Bank Public Library as the Doc Sayre house, now the site of the Whitfield Building. Jeremiah E. Sayre was born in Cape May in 1852 and graduated from Jefferson Medical College, Philadelphia. He bought the house on the corner of Broad and Wallace Streets where the Mercantile Bank Building was erected and moved the house. The history of this house is obscure, although it is apparent an older dwelling was given a Colonial Revival porch, with its pediment an extension of the attic.

Howard Whitfield built a Broad Street office on the west side, just north of the Strand Theatre, in the late 1920s. He became wealthy by manufacturing of a new type of carbon paper and supported charitable causes. He collected photographs of the old Red Bank area and residents, many of which appear in this book. One tree obscures a business casualty, a McDonald's that found town street traffic patterns were not fitting with suburban fast-food dining practices.

Peg Jordan identifies one of her ancestral homes as the John Bergen house on Broad Street. It occupied the northeast corner of Borden Street, renamed Linden Place, later the site of the Strand Theatre. The house was moved and today stands at 131 Spring Street, with its second-story bay removed.

The Strand Theatre opened on March 29, 1917, showing Mary Pickford in A *Poor Little Rich Girl*. It was located on the northeast corner of Broad Street and Linden Place, built as a motion picture theatre, but latter added vaudeville acts. The theatre seated 1,000 with a lobby and foyer capable of holding 250 people. The building still stands, extensively remodeled, first as a store and now as offices. This view is from the 1920s.

This scene north from Linden Places lengthens the perspective of the previous views and shows the Strand with a marquee. The year is 1934, with the film providing an easy dating aid.

Arthur Swift's building took the name of its store tenant, Knickerbocker Pharmacy, owned by Shrewsbury native Robert A. Van Derver. The business thrived for many years, but was sold at a bankruptcy sale in 1925. The sign of a notable office tenant is visible, Charles D. Warner. He was best known for his long service on Red Bank's board of education. Note the pleasing effect of the original street-level construction, the corner door and the store flush with the building line.

The prior First Methodist Church, built on the east side of Broad, near Front, was destroyed in the November 5, 1882 fire (see p. 10). A lot of the southwest corner on Broad and Monmouth Streets was purchased the next month and this church was erected. It was dedicated in March 1884. The church became surrounded by a growing business district, and long-contemplated moving. The building was demolished following the 1941 construction of the church at 247 Broad Street (see p. 35).

Stores were built on the First Methodist Church's lot after the 1941 demolition. The corner was long anchored by the Liggett-Rexall Drug store, with a large Schulte-United variety store surrounding it with an L-shaped plan. An indoor mall of small shops is on the site now. (The Dorn's Collection.)

A rapid rainfall totaling 5.5 inches on Saturday, July 29, 1961, overwhelmed the borough's sewers and inundated Broad Street from Harding Road to north of Canal Street. Canal Street was a popular spot for photographers for obvious reasons.

The George B. Sandt house at the southwest corner of Broad and Leroy Place was designed by William B. Tuthill. It was begun in 1888 and completed the next year on land of the former Anthony Reckless estate. The interior was octagonal. A large dome in the ceiling lit an 18-foot-wide hall. All rooms on the second floor could be reached from a gallery. Sandt sold it in 1898 to Henry and Mary Wood, who owned the house at the time of this *c.* 1910 postcard. The house was destroyed in 1923 to allow the erection of the Adelaide Court apartments.

The post office at the northeast corner of Broad and Canal Streets was completed *c.* 1931. It remained the town's main office until it was relocated to the present location at 171 Broad Street in November 1965.

The finest properties of the residential section north of Monmouth Street were the sizable estates of Henry Schroeder, James Peters, and Anthony Reckless (see p. 37). James H. Peters (1850–1898) married Mrs. Ella Green of Long Branch in 1890. He is pictured c. 1897 with his two children and, presumably, Mrs. Peters and a member of the family. (Collection of the Red Bank Public Library.)

After Peter's death, his house, one of the finest Italianate residences in Red Bank, was moved to the newly opened Peters Place. It is today home to Bernard Kellenyi and Associates, Architects, the firm having remodeled it into offices while retaining the building's residential character.

Architect Joseph Swannell (1858–1921) is standing at his drafting table at his Red Bank office with a picture of his magnum opus, St. James R.C. Church, on the wall. He was born in Brooklyn and spent his early career as a cabinet maker. Swannell opened an architects office in 1891 and had a lot of work until 1905, but little in the 1905–1915 period. He designed many houses, factories for Eisner, the Shrewsbury Christ Church parish hall, and the Red Bank armory. Swannell was employed by the T.A. Gillespie plant at Morgan during World War I.

The first St. James Roman Catholic Church was built at the southwest corner of Pearl and Wall Streets in the 1860s. The Romanesque Revival edifice on the west side of Broad Street was completed in 1894, designed by Joseph Swannell and built by T.H. Pryor & Son, Trenton. Early renderings of the church portray it with its present tower. However, the tower was not erected until 1911 after raising funds by subscription. The rectory, adjacent on the left, was replaced by the church's school in 1926, with a new rectory built on the site of the house barely visible at the right.

A c. 1920 postcard view of J. Lester Eisner's large, brick house built on the east side of Broad Street on the site of the former Maribah West home in 1916. It was the second largest and costliest house of its day. The 72-by-32-foot Georgian Revival with a 15-foot kitchen ell was designed by Newark architect Nathan Meyers. It was a residence only briefly (see below).

The new Methodist church was begun in 1941, designed by Wenner and Fink of Philadelphia and consecrated March 15, 1942. Its Colonial Revival style is said to have been inspired by the J. Lester Eisner house to which it is attached. The same firm designed Fellowship Hall, attached south of the Eisner house.

The Grace Methodist Church was organized March 22, 1880, at the home of Joseph W. Child, with early worship services held at a hall in the Haddon Building at Broad and White Streets. Their first edifice was erected at the northeast corner of Broad and Canal Streets and dedicated May 15, 1881. It was outgrown and this church was dedicated July 11, 1889, erected a block to the north at Broad and what was then Branch Avenue.

Henry Zobel bought the Grace Methodist Church property in 1925 and erected this automobile showroom and office building. The Red Bank Plan of 1931 illustrated the corner reflecting on the need to eliminate Harding Road's dangerous offset with Reckless Place. The showroom was converted to offices and Harding Road has been widened, but an offset still exists and the intersection requires considerable caution in crossing.

A 1920s postcard view of the former residence of Anthony Reckless. Reckless came to Red Bank in 1849, operating a store at Broad and Front Streets. He purchased a farm on upper Broad Street and built this Italianate house designed by J.P. Huber in 1862. He is best known as the major figure behind the New York and Long Branch Railroad, a line that he served as president and in other capacities for many years. Reckless died in 1889. His property was purchased by lawyer Fred Hope, who developed and opened Reckless Place. Hope sold the residence to the Red Bank Womens Club in 1921, who still occupy the premises as a club house and residence. (Collection of Michael Steinhorn.)

The Presbyterians moved south of the business district when they erected this edifice on the southwest corner of Broad Street and Reckless Place in 1911. The impressive stone structure, shown in this c. 1912 postcard, lasted only forty-one years, as the business district expanded and the church sought ample space. This building was demolished in December, 1952, as the present church was being built on the Elkus estate on Tower Hill.

The Theodore White house stands at 286 Broad Street, at the northwest corner with Bergen Place. It is a fine Second Empire example, built around the mid-1870s by one of Red Bank's largest real estate investors. It was then outside the limits of the newly organized town. White had extensive holdings, much of them to the west of his house. He coined the term "west side" for the emerging neighborhood, once called "Texas" to reflect its distant and unsettled state. The house is now offices.

The Red Bank Elks lodge was founded in 1911, occupying rented space on Broad Street, prior to their purchasing a house on Front Street. They built this enormous Broad Street building to a design by Vincent Eck. Its cost and a lack of business during the depression resulted in its loss. The building was a USO facility during World War II. The Progressive Life Insurance Company purchased it in 1945, occupying the building as its home office for many years. The former Elks lodge has been remodeled into medical offices.

The Sarah C. Hadden house at 310 Broad Street is a late work of architect Joseph Swannell, built in 1915. It was a Colonial Revival design, then the predominate style in the county and country. However, it employs a red tile roof more characteristic in this area of Italian Renaissance Revival, with examples on Broad Street, such as the one below. Nicknamed Elm Court, the house is now the Adams Memorial Home.

Ernest A. Arend was one of Monmouth County's leading architects for the first third of this century. His career spanned the concurrent existence of the Colonial and Period Revivals. His diverse practice included domestic examples designed in both styles, favoring brick Georgian Revivals and stucco Italian Renaissance Revivals. He chose the latter for his house built in 1910 on the northeast corner of Broad Street and Bergen Place, a site now occupied by a bank. (From the October 10, 1916 *Asbury Park Press* Pictorial Supplement.)

George Sandt owned this Tudor Revival house at Broad Street's northeast corner with Pinckney Road. It was moved to the Silverwhite Gardens development in nearby Little Silver to clear its lot for the apartments below.

Les Gertrudes Apartments was built in 1928 at the northeast corner of Broad Street and Pinckney Road for owner John McDonald to a design by K. Mac M. Towner. Both the architect and the builder, H.M. Steelman, were from Asbury Park. The place was built with forty apartments from three to six rooms. Rents at the time ran from $95 to $150.

Two

Front Street

The Globe Hotel, located on the south side of Front Street, a block east of Broad, was built as a dwelling by Robert Hart in 1840, according to Franklin Ellis' 1885 *History of Monmouth County* and enlarged for use as a hotel by Tobias Hendrickson, its buyer in 1844. The building was further enlarged, probably on several occasions. This gathering, probably in the late nineteenth century, may be typical of many there, as the hotel functioned as an all-purpose community center. The hotel was destroyed by fire December 19, 1936, in a massive blaze that left the bar and dining room standing.

This *c*. 1910 view east on Front about a block west of Broad appears congested, largely due to balconies on two buildings on the north side (left). The cola sign marks the five one-story stores separating the more substantial buildings. The trees in the background mark the start of the residential section after a one-block East Front Street business district.

J. Trafford Allen erected a store at Front and Maple Streets (the latter then Divisian Street) in 1875. This is the oldest photograph in the book, from a Pach stereocard. It shows Allen's lumber yard by the water and the shore line east to the area of the steamboat dock.

Front Street at Wharf Avenue looking east around 1910. The corner of the Hendrickson and Applegate Building at the right and a barely discernable Lamb Building on the left are the only recognizable structures still standing.

J. Trafford Allen lived to age ninety-five, retiring from his hardware business only two years prior to his death in 1930. It thrived when commercial maritime traffic was heavy, as Allen was a major supplier to the ships. He also had extensive Red Bank real estate holdings. (From the *Register* of November 9, 1904.)

Sylvan Siegel bought a lot from the William B. Parker estate when Harrison Avenue was opened c. 1899. That year he hired Joseph Swannell (see p. 34) to design this large house with elaborate appointments, expecting he would remain there for the rest of his life. He was forced to sell within ten years, and the place was bought by noted Red Bank photographer Joseph Dickopf, who owned it only two years before selling it to Edouard Methot.

This early-1940s photograph by Ed Kemble shows that gas stations were the only intrusion on the residential section of East Front Street. The Stout house (see p. 26) is in the foreground, while Georgie Hazard's Burton Hall School is obscured in the row behind it.

This is part of a panoramic photograph that includes the top of p. 44. The view shows the rural character of eastern River Road, Front Street's identity east of the Throckmorton Bridge, early in the century. On the right is the driveway to Rose Hall, the name given to the Warren Sillcocks house while it was owned by June's grandfather Homer Methot, in honor of her grandmother's distinguished rose plantings. (Photograph lent by June Methot.)

This attractive Queen Anne-style house was probably built by Warren Sillcocks shortly after his 1891 purchase of the land. The Methots sold it to Martin and Elizabeth Nill who, in conjunction with Thomas and Viola Jardine, opened Alston Court and developed their sides of it, the west and east respectively. The house still stands at 20 Alston Court.

Kridel's sign effectively shields the old frame store at the southeast corner of Front and Broad in this *c.* 1912 postcard. The brick stores at left are still standing, but those west of Wharf Avenue are gone. The familiar and still standing Hendrickson and Applegate Building is behind Kridel's and the familiar, but destroyed, Globe Hotel is behind it. Note the sign for the old Lyric Theatre.

Jacob Degenring owned the Germania Hotel on the north side of Front Street, opposite Broad, when this view was taken around 1910. He also had an interest in the H.G. Degenring bottling plant behind the hotel. (The Dorn's Collection.)

James Grover, born in Red Bank in 1869, was the head salesman for M.M. Davidson's before opening his store on Front Street. He later became a salesman for New York clothing firms. The picture is likely from an early-twentieth-century carnival celebration. The lender, Donald Magee, notes the subject is his grandfather, Eugene Magee.

Jacob B. Rue claimed to have the largest and best-equipped auto station and boat launch along the Shrewsbury River (the old name of the Navesink) after the 1908 erection of this building at 32 West Front Street. It was a 50-by-128-foot garage designed by William A. Shoemaker, with a storage capacity of about 50 cars. A machine shop building and boat launch were behind it on a property that ran from street to river.

The John W. Stout house at 41 East Front Street still possessed many of its early features *c.* 1950. The most notable loss is the tower. The house is believed to have been started *c.* 1855 and expanded several times. Stout had a tomato canning factory behind Wharf Avenue a short distance to the west of his house. (An Ed Kemble photograph.)

G.A. Van Brunt, fish seller, is in the center, while his assistant displays one with a "look how fresh our stock is" pose. The building at left is Hendrickson and Applegates, now Kislins. One of Red Bank's earliest stores was a frame structure at the southeast corner of Broad and Front Streets. A piece of it can be seen in this turn-of-the-century photograph.

The Second National Bank organized in 1875 and opened in this building on the north side of Front Street opposite the Globe Hotel, on May 12, 1875. The bank absorbed by merger the Red Bank Trust Company, which had earlier merged with the First National Bank, and moved to Broad Street. (Collection of the Red Bank Public Library.)

The George R. Lamb Building is a fine, little-altered example of Commercial Italianate architecture. It was built for a liquor dealer in 1893, the date inscribed on the cornice. Its underuse for storage makes one wary about the future of this well-preserved early store.

This *c.* 1905 Foxwell photograph shows the north side of Front Street opposite Broad decorated for a firemen's parade. The Sheridan Hotel was operated by Fred Frick who sold it in 1908 to focus on his new theatre (see p. 71). It was remodeled, with a floor apparently removed, and a new brick face added in 1930. Hesse's is the restored Downtown Cafe.

William Cullington emigrated from England in 1853 and learned the cigar maker's trade in Connecticut. He succeeded his father, who founded John Cullington & Son in 1873, upon the latter's retirement in 1894. Two quality 5¢ cigars were their specialty: "Cuban Commerce" and "Searchlight." (From the June 1904 *Industrial Recorder*.)

Oscar Hesse began his ice cream business in 1879. His building at 8 West Front Street was built after the 1881 fire, with this interior shown in a c. 1910 postcard. He retired in 1924, selling the business to his son Joseph. The frames on the wall contained stuffed birds. Ice cream parlors appear nearly defunct in the east. All in the author's memory had a characteristic fragrance, one not replicated in similar contemporary shops. One wonders what combination of products produced it. (Collection of Edwin F. Banfield.)

Were these clippings from the workbench or floor? No drugs, but what about nicotine? Oh, wait, the ad dates from 1903 (the *Register* of April 15). The tobacco industry has a long record of misleading advertisements.

William W. Conover, a well-liked, astute real estate investor who supported public improvement and private charity, built this fine Second Empire house at 81 East Front Street, probably in the late 1860s. He was a strong abolitionist and was called "Black Bill," reflecting his hatred of slavery, a nickname that became an honorific. Its substance is apparent when compared with the corner of Henry Nevius' similarly-styled house at the right, one demolished for a professional building in 1955. (An Ed Kemble photograph c. early 1950s.)

The dark blue surface with white trim painting is so familiar at this location that many may be surprised to find that there was an earlier scheme. Bright colors with white trim have become popular color schemes for Victorian-era buildings in the recent past, but historical accuracy is questionable. Period buildings often had a light, dull, warm appearance with dark trim, often a variant of the main surface's color. Paint remains a subject posing a considerable research challenge. The building is now Riverview Medical Center's Century House.

Blaisdell Residence, on the Shrewsbury, Red Bank, N. J.

The Frank Blaisdell house, built *c.* 1890s on the river near the present Fair Haven border, is best remembered for its interior finish with a variety of woods. Blaisdell, a lumber dealer, chose carefully and at length, its construction spanning two and one-half years. The *Register* described the interior on May 10, 1911, when Mrs. Blaisdell placed the house on the market. It contained a maple dining room, birch library, mahogany parlor and music room, butternut billiard room, white oak halls, and two cherry bedrooms, with several rooms in red oak, including the kitchen and butler's pantry. This view is from a *c.* 1905 postcard. The house was demolished in the early 1970s.

Evelyn Leavens, distinguished Red Bank artist, taking a youthful leap in the early 1940s onto the beach in front of the Blaisdell house with an early expression of her philosophy, "Why grow-up?". It is not a bad philosophy as she looks back a half-century later, happy, well-adjusted, and doing all what she chooses to do.

Viola Jardine was active with the Better Homes Week program begun by the national office of the women's club movement. She planned one house in nearby Harris Park in 1926, and purchased plans for this Tudor Revival, which was built on a lot she sold in 1928, while developing the eastern side of Alston Court. See the opposite page for the advertised water privileges. (From the *Register* of September 5, 1928.)

The house in the above ad was built for Eric Leavens at 5 Alston Court, begun in 1928 and finished the next year. It retains its original appearance.

Alston Court was developed in the late 1920s by the Thomas Jardines and the Martin Nills, the east and west sides respectively. They provided access to the river in their deeds of sale through a narrow right of way through an agreement that is on file in the county deed records. That strip is overgrown now, but was clearly delineated *c.* 1940 when Evelyn Leavens was walking her dog there. Knowing Evelyn, she probably would have faced the camera had she known the photograph would be published a half-century later.

The Leavens play house is a landmark of its type. It is over sixty years old and has been moved at least four times, a condition that generally denies historic register eligibility.

Dr. Charles Hubbard, a dentist, was born in Tinton Falls, the son of a doctor. He studied dentistry with Dr. J.B. Brown in Brooklyn and opened a Red Bank office. He built this Second Empire house on East Front Street, opposite the Trinity Episcopal Church in 1868, seen here in an image from the 1878 *Woolman & Rose*.

Dr. Hubbard's house was aging but still serviceable in the early 1950s. It was one of three contiguous houses converted into the Bluffs, which added new multiple dwellings closer to the water in the early 1980s. Deteriorating conditions resulted in the virtual reconstruction of the buildings. (An Ed Kemble photograph.)

The house at 58 West Front Street is one of Red Bank's oldest, and is now one of its most urgent preservation projects. A fine Greek Revival example, it was probably built in the 1830s or '40s. It is today associated with Dr. and Mrs. Walter Rullman, who purchased it in 1919, making additions and alterations designed by Fred Truex in 1925.

William Applegate's house formerly stood on Maple Avenue. It was moved to Front Street on the site of the former Baptist Church around 1900, when improvements, including the three-sided porch the port-cochere and the three-story tower, were made. It, too, was substantially reconstructed in the early 1980s during the building of the Bluffs.

The Italian Villa-style Stacey Pitcher house was likely built in the 1860s, with the dormers added later. According to the *Register* of March 14, 1906, the year of Sigmund Eisner's purchase, it was known as the Starr house as a Professor Starr kept a boys' school there. Eisner took down the tower and clad the building in stucco in 1921. In 1937, his heirs donated the house to the borough for a library, now known as the Eisner Memorial Library. (The Dorn's Collection.)

Red Bank's public library, the Eisner Memorial Library, was expanded greatly by building an extension on the river side of the house. It was designed by noted Newark architect William E. Lehman, constructed in 1967–68 and re-opened September 16, 1968, giving the library about 15,000 square feet. One can use the library for years without viewing its north elevation. Now that you have conveniently seen it here, take the path from their new parking lot and see the rest of the building and a fine view of the river.

Dr. Smith Cutter was the son of Ford Cutter, a veteran of the Battle of Monmouth. He had earlier lived in New York and Shrewsbury and moved to Red Bank c. 1850, probably building his house shortly thereafter, as it appears on the 1851 Lightfoot map. Dr. Smith's obituary indicated he was the only doctor to go to New York City's yellow fever area in 1822. This superior, three-story Italianate house with a cupola, must have been one of the largest in Red Bank when built east of the Rullman place. (Collection Monmouth County Historical Association.)

The Riverside Gardens Apartments were built in 1927 on part of the former Cutter lot. It was designed by C.T. Friis, who had a personal interest, taking an apartment there. The building was damaged by fire while vacant in 1988 and demolished. It is the site of a borough park, also called Riverside Gardens.

Trinity Episcopal Church, 65 West Front Street, was dedicated May 13, 1851. It was then a mission of Christ Church, Shrewsbury, becoming a parish several years later. The church has been altered several times. It is shown on the 1851 Lightfoot map in a drawing with its full tower. However, another photograph taken some years later pictures only half the tower seen in this *c.* 1910 postcard, suggesting the tower was built in two stages.

Open flames and extensive Christmas greens in Trinity Episcopal Church, *c.* 1880s, makes one wary of the fire hazard. The church was extensively damaged by fire in 1968 on Easter but rebuilt within a year.

Sigmund Eisner's house at the left (with the tower), now the library, helps establish the perspective for this *c.* 1915 view east. The William Applegate house is adjacent and the cupola of the Dr. Smith Cutter house is barely discernable amidst the trees.

The Red Bank Opera House, a theatre built by Charles Gorden Allen in 1883, occupied a large lot on the south side of Front Street west of Maple Avenue. It burned on June 24, 1905. The private collections of actors were lost, part of the total destruction of its contents. French's Central Hotel, adjacent on the corner, was saved to await its proposed fate, demolition for a proposed retail facility.

The Baptist Church in Red Bank was founded in July 1844. This Greek Revival structure, located on Front Street near todays library, was dedicated July 17, 1849. After the construction of the Maple Avenue church, this one was sold to the Calvary Baptist Church, an African-American congregation, and moved to Bridge Avenue. There it burned in 1902. The restored church was later destroyed in a storm. (From an illustration in the *Historical Souvenir of the Seventy-Fifth Anniversary of The First Baptist Church, Red Bank, N.J.*, 1914.)

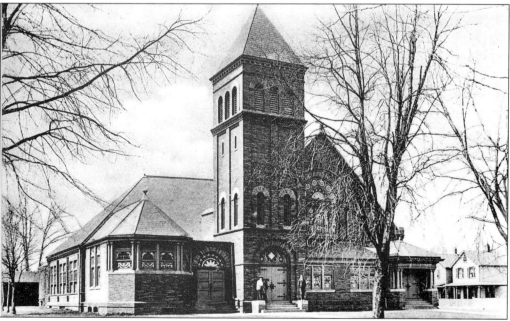

The First Baptist Church replaced the above modest structure with a large, brick Romanesque Revival edifice designed by New York architect William B. Tuthill, who also designed Carnegie Hall. Its 72-foot-high square tower with pyramidal roof made it one of the tallest, if not the tallest, structure in Red Bank when it was built. This postcard view is *c.* 1910.

Three

The Waterfront

Initial speculation on the boaters' unhappy faces dwelled on their being forced to wear their good duds on the outing, thus inhibiting their fun. However, slow film and posing fashion of a century ago are more likely reasons for their dull demeanor.

This *c.* 1905 view of the Navesink River fronting on Riverside Avenue reflects its character as a residential street of private houses. That character began to change in the late 1920s with the erection of the Molly Pitcher Hotel and the Twin Gables Apartments, and had disappeared by the 1970s.

The same private residences remained on Riverside Avenue in the mid-1950s. At the left, houses stood where an office and apartment stand now. The Molly Pitcher Hotel (center) and Twin Gables Apartments (right) anchor the street that in time would be dominated by multiple brick dwellings and institutional buildings.

Union Street remained a waterfront residential locale well into the 1940s before Riverview Hospital, the house on the left, expanded, in time replacing the structures to the east (on the right). (An Ed Kemble photograph.)

The first Coopers Bridge that spanned the Navesink River connecting Middletown and Red Bank was built c. 1835. The present concrete bridge, part of Highway 35, opened in 1926. This intermediate span is from a c. 1905 postcard. The Coopers owned the property on the north bank, or Middletown, side.

The Monmouth Boat Club, founded in 1879, grew rapidly, enabling it to expand its 1880 20-by-50-foot clubhouse. This 1884 view reflects a new second-story expansion and a 25-foot one-story addition on the river end. Commodore Joseph T. Burrowes is the white-bearded gentleman with Dr. Edwin Field, organizer of the club, to his right.

The growing Monmouth Boat Club built a new clubhouse in 1895, selecting a three-story structure in view of their narrow lot. This view is from a c. 1910 postcard. The scene today shows a major 1930 addition on the west (on the right). The site's stature as long-time capital of maritime sport on the river was recognized in 1994 with its listing on the New Jersey Register of Historic Places.

Canoeing became popular on the Navesink River in the 1880s. Local canoeists organized a club in 1887, using William L. Sneden's Riverside Avenue boathouse for a meeting site and storage facility.

The short-lived Shrewsbury River Yacht Club built this extravagance as a clubhouse on the Navesink River, east of Prospect Avenue, in 1893. They might have called themselves the Fair Haven Yacht Club as most of its organizers were from that part of Shrewsbury Township that became Fair Haven Borough in 1912. The building was designed by D.C. Ernst Laub, supervised by his co-architect Robert D. Chandler, and built by William C. Brown of Red Bank. The club lasted less than ten years, with the property sold for residential development.

Seeing and being seen were non-strenuous activities on the iced-over Navesink as these two attractive women demonstrated around the turn of the century. (The Dorn's Collection.)

The relative roles of sailing and steam vessels and the railroad in developing Red Bank would make an interesting scholarly study. Sailing ships helped raise the town from infancy in its early years, with some lasting into the early twentieth century, carrying less costly bulk cargo. June Methot's landmark *Up and Down the River* identifies these schooners as the *Jordan Wooley* and *Toledo*, shown in a *c*. 1890 picture at the Steamboat Dock. (The Dorn's Collection.)

Charles Irwin's yacht works, which judging by the pre-1907 date of this postcard was probably his first yard, was replaced by an expanded facility in 1909. The yards were rebuilt again and today remain an important riverfront enterprise.

Boat building was an early career of William H.R. White, who would become a real estate developer and mayor of Red Bank. Maritime leanings may have come from his father who began a boat rental business c. 1884. When The Industrial Recorder published this view in 1904, White was prideful of the power launch The Yankee Boy just finished for Benjamin S. Payne. White's popularity may be inferred from this Democrat consistently receiving heavy majorities in a Republican town.

The Red Bank Yacht Club was formed in 1896, electing New York brewer and Navesink River Road summer resident J. Christian Hupfel commodore. They built this clubhouse on a 40-by-60-foot float. Their first race was held May 29, 1897; it was won by Harry Knapp's *Nereid*.

The interior of the above clubhouse. Note the flags of the great maritime nations, including Switzerland.

Fred Frick's Lyceum opened September 3, 1906, with a performance of Shakespeare's *The Merry Wives of Windsor*, with Louis James performing as Sir John Falstaff. The Monmouth Boat Club (right) provides a reminder of the location of the no-longer standing theatre. It was designed by William A. Shoemaker and built on the former site of John W. Stout's tomato canning factory. The Lyceum presented vaudeville and motion pictures.

Both the Monmouth Boat Club (right) and the North Shrewsbury Ice Boat & Yacht Club (left) are visible west of the borough tennis courts, built on the site of Frick's Lyceum.

Ice boating on the Navesink is centered at the North Shrewsbury Ice Boat & Yacht Club, located at Union Street and Boat Club Court. Founded in 1880, members race about eight classes of modern boats and compete for several trophies awarded by the Club. These events are open to competitors from a wide circle of the ice boat racing world.

Cal Smith, in his book *Ice boating* (1962) noted that Charles and William Merritt of Chelsea, New York, built the first lateen-rigged ice boat, an adaptation of the Dhow sail that was intended to improve steering control. Robert D. Chandler, also an architect, built such a vessel in 1884 for James B. Weaver. The *Scud* is shown here, perhaps around the time of its big victory in its first race in January 1885.

Ice boats encounter little resistance on the ice and can travel "faster than the wind." Reclining in the cockpit for maneuvering the tiller can produce a closeness to the ice hard for the uninitiated to imagine, including the author.

Skate sailing involves a person on ice skates using a kite-like device in the same basic manner as an ice boat. Skaters can reach speeds of 50–60 miles per hour. This view is a c. 1913 ice carnival on the Navesink.

A view of the Merchants Steamboat Company's *Albertina* from a *c.* 1910 postcard. Built in 1882, it was 165-feet long, and was extended 9 feet later in the 1880s. It plied the Navesink River into the 1930s. Captain Charles B. Parsons in a 1905 paper presented to the Monmouth County Historical Association reflected on how railroad-induced development stimulated business to replace lost freight traffic. Horses, carriages, and moving vans of the city summer residents provided considerable profitable traffic.

An ad from the April 30, 1890 *Register*. One wonders if the vessel was still "new and elegant" in its ninth season. Captain Charles E. Throckmorton was an owner of the Merchants Steamboat Company, having purchased his father's interest with his brother, and having taken the helm of the *Albertina* from the former. He took no nonsense on board, having secured the largest fine in the county for swearing in a case against Joseph Bennett. The fine totaled $15.50 at the statutory rate of 50¢ per oath. Obviously, someone counted.

A c. 1915 postcard view of the *Sea Bird,* the longest running steamer on the New York–Navesink River route. It began in 1866, the year of its construction, and continued for sixty years. This 187-foot-long vessel was built by Edward Minturn, a New Yorker with a summer home on the Navesink at Rocky Point, and Moses Taylor, who had one of the most important of the Elberon cottages. The *Sea Bird* sustained a serious fire in 1867, but returned to sea the following year.

The warehouse of the Merchants Steamboat Company at the foot of Wharf Avenue provided short-term storage for steamer cargo. This view is from a *c.* 1910 postcard.

Eelers cut holes about a yard in diameter and shoved the block under the ice to preclude its interference with skaters and ice boats. They then prodded the bottom of the river with long-handled spears, up to 30 feet in length. Eels hibernating in soft, shallow mud were caught on the prongs and raised promptly to minimize the chances of their escaping (see the the *Register of* February 1, 1911, for an article on ice eeling). The holes are now restricted by law to 10 inches in diameter. (Collection of the Red Bank Public Library.)

The often-illustrated Molly Pitcher Hotel, 88 Riverside Avenue, was opened in 1929. This picture is a rendering from the architect Nathan Harris. Its Georgian Revival style was quite popular at the height of the Colonial Revival and is still expressed in contemporary forms in Monmouth County. The name was taken from the Revolutionary War figure who gained recognition for her actions at the Battle of Monmouth in June 1778. (Collection of Michael Steinhorn.)

This view of the Duffy cottage appeared in a May 24, 1899 *Register* ad announcing an auction to settle the Duffy estate. It was located on Locust Street, on the banks of the Navesink. Mystery surrounds the place, including the spelling of Ann Duffy's name. This may be Mansion House, a former resort, that was reported destroyed by fire in May 1906. A house with a large second-story balcony is on the site now, but it does not otherwise match the Duffy cottage.

A 1930s postcard view of Stalder's Recreation Center, which catered to a variety of activities including banquets, private parties, bowling, boating, and fishing. It was located on the Navesink shore, adjacent to and west of Coopers Bridge, Highway 35. It later became the Riverside Motel.

Henry Hoffmire built this substantial frame house at 74 Shrewsbury Avenue *c.* 1850. He was a baker and political figure. It passed from the family in 1909, later serving as a school. An antique shop opened in 1945, giving the place its current name, the SOHO House. After several years of vacancy, the house was destroyed in 1995.

Miss Mary Cornell of Middletown's Cornell Preparatory School and Miss Louise Peacock of Miss Hewitt's School, New York City, opened the Cornell-Peacock School at the Hoffmire house in 1923. This picture from the 1920s was taken at a student's home. One wonders about the nature of the event and why some children are sleeveless while others are in topcoats.

Four
People, Places, and Events

The Red Bank Arrowsmith Post of the Grand Army of the Republic in 1885, presumably at their summer fair. If that year was similar to the 1883 fair, described in detail in the *Register*, it spanned several days, with the men selling various wares and edibles to the public. The fair even published a newspaper, the *Daily Gazette*. (Collection of the Red Bank Public Library.)

Senator Henry M. Nevius (left) and Edmund Wilson, two of Red Bank's most estimable lawyers, shortly after their link in partnership in 1888. Nevius, a Civil War veteran, enlisted with a Michigan outfit, where he had been a university student. He was long active with the GAR, serving as state president, and was a judge and county prosecutor. Wilson studied law at Columbia; he became a highly-regarded trial lawyer, and served as New Jersey attorney general. He was interested in education, serving on the Red Bank and state boards of education, and was involved in local philanthropic matters. He was the father of the writer of the same name. (Collection of the Red Bank Public Library.)

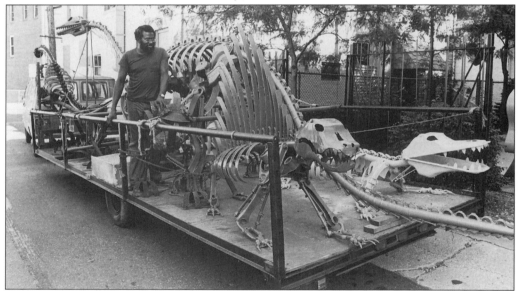

Jim Gary was born 1939 in Florida and raised in Colts Neck where he began his Iron Butterfly Art Studio and Gallery. A metal sculptor who used junk yards as his art supply stores, Gary early specialized in dinosaurs fashioned from automobile parts. He relocated to Red Bank in 1970 and is shown here on a special trailer used to transport the sculptures. The breadth of his acclaim can be appreciated from his exhibitions at science museums as well as a long list of traditional art sites.

This *c.* 1950 class of Mrs. O'Shea's Red Bank Business Institute seems quite pleased to be graduating. Mrs. O'Shea, who ran the school in her home at Broad Street and Peters Place, wears the symbol of authority, the hat, and what was then a token of advancing years, the eyeglasses. The school operated from 1926 to 1965. The picture was lent by Ann Jacoby, whose mother, Lois Pennington Gryson, is to the teacher's left.

The Riverside Gun Club in 1890. Their star gunner was Albert L. Ivins, virtually unbeatable locally and a winner of state titles, too. (Collection of the Red Bank Public Library.)

The Ku Klux Klan was active along the shore in the 1920s with headquarters at Elkwood Park. Red Bank's chapter was organized in 1923. The KKK sought a parade permit in 1925, which was denied by Mayor William H.R. White. The borough council overruled him, but the event was turned into an Armistice Day parade with participation by many organizations. The KKK had insidious means of disguising their hateful purpose, such as visiting churches en masse, while hooded, and leaving above average sums in the collection plate. Their ways remind us that those who disguise evil with false pretenses of high ideals are the most dangerous of all. (Collection of the Shrewsbury Historical Society.)

A 1928 photograph of Grace Blackwell with a Monmouth County Organizations for Social Services ambulance, outside their new offices on Pearl Street, built the prior year to resemble a large house. The group, now known as the Visiting Nurse Association of Monmouth County, remained there until 1950 when it relocated to the former Cecil Conover factory on North Riverside Avenue. (Collection of the Red Bank Public Library.)

The Red Bank *Register* was founded in 1878. It quickly grew and prospered. At its peak, it was arguably the best country weekly in America. Early local news gathering involved an editor traveling to various local towns, initially on a bicycle, to learn firsthand what was happening. The process was swifter by the time Layton Webster (left) and Frank Long operated their Linotypes, particularly for the former, whose machine was run by teletype.

The *Register* was located on Broad Street for many years, most of them at #40–42, which included its press as well as the composing room and business office. Ed Egan (left) and John Mattoccia are printing in 1953, three years before the press operation was relocated to a new building at West and Chestnut Streets.

Dick Kirby, a leather craftsman neighbor from the east side of Wharf Avenue, recalled Jim Lang, long-time proprietor of the Union Bar, seen here *c.* 1944 talking with a produce huckster. The place, known variously as the Union Hotel and Old Union House, was sold for restoration in 1952, later burned, was reopened and closed. Hotel use diminished after the Frick Lyceum closed *c.* 1910s. (An Ed Kemble photograph.)

Cal Kennal is standing outside the D.C. Wood leather shop on the east side of Wharf Avenue *c.* 1944. The building was demolished for a parking lot, but Dick Kirby, the proprietor of the business relocated on Linden Place, recalled, "I learned more from him than anyone else." Kennal's stitching horse is still in the shop. (An Ed Kemble photograph.)

A public produce exchange developed on the green around Wharf Avenue in the nineteenth century. Its wholesale prices were often a measure of the market. Ed Kemble believed the buyer at the right was the last huckster when he photographed this scene in 1944. The identity of the merchant has been disputed. Some claim he is John Galatro, who leased the building later converted into a dining room of the adjacent Union House.

Sam Drum was an itinerant fish peddler, who, often dressed in a military uniform, would walk through town, beating his drum, singing, and selling fish. Later in life his verbal repertoire included mumblings about salvation, which may or may not have been attributed to his decline of sanity. He died in February 1905 at the Trenton insane asylum at about age seventy. (Collection of the Red Bank Public Library.)

This late 1940s aerial view east along Monmouth Street shows subtle, but significant, change. The Eisner factory is at the lower left, while the railroad station is at the lower right. Broad Street runs along the top with the Strand Theatre building, now an office, in the center. Note

the size of the Count Basie Theatre, most of it behind the street facade. Station parking seems casual. The number of coal dealers reflects the significance of the fuel at that time. What changes strike you?

The transformation of Monmouth Street from residential to business, a process that accelerated in the first decade of this century, is still suggested by the number of store fronts that cover the dwellings behind them. This c. 1908 postcard view from is probably west of Maple Avenue.

The Red Bank Post Office moved from the Broad Street Mercantile Bank Building to George Hance Patterson's new building on Sunday, December 7, 1910. It was located adjacent to his house, also relocated from Broad Street. The annual rent then was $1,800. (The Dorn's Collection.)

The Robert Allen house was located on the west side of Broad Street between Monmouth and White Streets. It was purchased by George Hance Patterson, Allen's son-in-law, shortly before he moved it in 1905 to its now familiar location at 30 Monmouth Street. Patterson then built the stores on the top of p. 24. The building was converted to retail use in late 1971 and now houses the Dubliner House restaurant.

The man may be L.S. Chasey, who founded the Monmouth Rustic Manufacturing Company in 1886. This locale was 172 Monmouth Street, with the product line including settees, bird houses, flower stands, arm chairs, baskets, and summer houses.

This *c.* 1905 postcard view reflects a still residential character of the north side of Monmouth Street looking east from the town hall. The YMCA is beyond the hall.

Red Bank's Romanesque Revival police station, designed by local architect Robert D. Chandler, was built in 1892 as the Shrewsbury Township Hall. It contained a 24-by-40-foot court room on the first floor and a 42-by-52-foot public hall on the second floor with a 600 person seating capacity. The clock in the tower was paid by public subscription. The building served as Red Bank's borough hall after its separation from the Township until the former telephone building at 32 Monmouth Street was converted to its municipal building in 1958. This is a *c.* 1910 postcard view. The building is listed on the National Register of Historic Places.

The monument *Handing Down Old Glory* was made in Barre, Vermont, and installed by Frank J. Manson on the borough hall grounds. It was dedicated on Memorial Day, May 30, 1926, a gift from the Red Bank firemen to the town.

The Young Men's Christian Association bought a building adjacent to the Township Hall that included a store, public hall, and bowling alley. They remodeled the building extensively and dedicated it in July 1905. This postcard dates shortly from thereafter. The building was converted to a store in 1926.

Ed von Kattengell established an automobile garage and sales agency on the southeast corner of Monmouth Street and Maple Avenue in 1905. At the time of this c. 1908 photograph, it was able to store seventy cars and provide sleeping rooms and other facilities for chauffeurs. Early autos sold included the Pope-Toledo, the EMF, the Oakland (in this view), and later, the Cadillac. (The Dorn's Collection.)

This A&P self-service super market was hailed at its June 9, 1938, opening as a large, up-to-date store featuring the latest in retail equipment and practices. It was located on the south side of Monmouth Street, near Pearl. When it closed in 1975, the store was considered small and obsolete. A run of nearly forty years is lengthy in an industry that constantly and extensively evolves. Red Bank is left with only one super market in 1995.

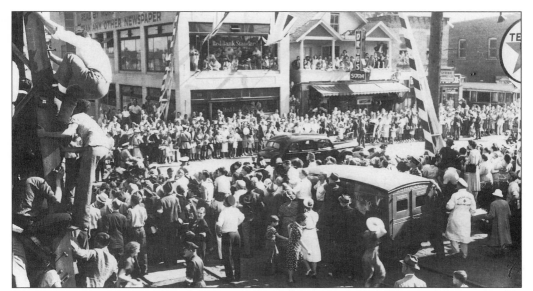

King George VI and Queen Elizabeth visited Red Bank on June 10, 1939. Their visit ostensibly stemmed from President Roosevelt's desire for them to see New York City via a harbor arrival. One wonders if security was also a consideration, with a desire to avoid a railroad tunnel and the limited aviation facilities of the day. Crowds were enormous. This view is on Monmouth Street, just east of the railroad station. The tall building is the five-story structure erected in 1927 by contractors S.S. Thompson & Co. for themselves and later occupied by the Red Bank Standard. (A Dan Dorn photograph from the Dorn's Collection.)

The often-reproduced arrival of the King and Queen at the railroad station greeted by Mayor English (the name a coincidence) is contrasted with the view most Red Bankers received, inset in the corner. Their motorcade traveled rapidly over Tower Hill and via Rumson Road en route to Sandy Hook for their departure by naval warship. It contained numerous large black sedans. When asked how she knew this one contained the royal visitors, photographer Evelyn Leavens replied, "That's the one people pointed towards."

A parade of decorated automobiles was a part of the annual summer carnival, a civic self-promotion and entertainment staple of the early 1900s. It appears that the flowers and the adult occupants of the car have been in the sun too long.

Boro Buses was organized in 1922 to replace trolley service discontinued that year. Although pressed for equipment at the outset, the line was well-received and soon bought three comfortable Packard buses. They also used Macks, with this vehicle, perhaps from the late 1920s, unidentified. (The Dorn's Collection.)

The Raritan & Delaware Bay Railroad began at Port Monmouth, Middletown, and crossed the Navesink River, entering Red Bank east of Coopers Bridge at the site of the power lines. Their passenger and freight depots were on Morford Place. Initially limited by the difficulties of its steamer connections at Port Monmouth, by 1870 the line was a major factor in the late-century acceleration of Red Bank's growth. Photographs of the station are rare. This view is from the July 26, 1878 *The Daily Graphic* of New York.

The New York and Long Branch Railroad's opening trip for invited guests was made on June 25, 1875. Public traffic began July 7, 1875. Rail service improved considerably as the "all land route" to New York provided access via a short ferry ride from Jersey City as opposed to the steamer trip from Port Monmouth. A temporary depot was erected and replaced in November 1875 by this station. Similar stations were erected at Matawan and Branchport.

The 1930 erection of a tower in the Red Bank railroad yard for the high tension power line.

A view of the Red Bank railroad yard from Chestnut Street in 1930

Alec Finch captured this view of the turntable in the Red Bank railroad yard in 1950, a reminder of the town's former status as a major rail center. Two Central Railroad of New Jersey Type 677 freight engines are at center and right, while the third is an unidentified Pennsylvania Railroad locomotive. The turntable was located east of the former New Jersey Southern tracks, behind the block between Catherine and Leonard Streets.

A northbound Pennsylvania Railroad train was derailed on Friday, March 19, 1909, due to spreading of the rails. Conductor John Moore was reported the only person injured, receiving cuts and bruises when thrown from the platform of the passenger coach nearest the baggage car. The *Register* of March 24, 1909, reported that Charles Foxwell "was on the scene early and got several fine pictures." This is one.

Three generations of John Stilwell Applegates are shown in an unidentified house. Seated is Senator Applegate, a lawyer, whose public career began as school superintendent, and included service in the state senate and positions on many boards. Kneeling is his son, a Harvard-educated lawyer with a significant Red Bank practice, who also served on numerous local boards. The youngest Applegate was born in 1901, permitting a c. 1910 inferred date for the picture. (Collection of the Red Bank Public Library.)

Playing hearts was an old winter custom in the back of Phil Stoffel's Broad Street cigar store. Since five of the seven are wearing hats, one presumes it was chilly there. They are, from left to right: Borden Wolcutt, Pop Bloomberg, Mr. Updyke, Arch Antonides, Arch Haveland, Bill Cole, and Will Hockma. It's been said that Antonides and Haveland were arch rivals. The picture and identities are from the Collection of the Red Bank Public Library.

The Red Bank Airport was built in 1926 by Air View, Inc., just beyond the borough border on the west side of Shrewsbury Avenue in today's Tinton Falls. Jack Casey was the aviator for the firm, which operated an aerial photography business. This view is from a c. 1940 postcard. A number of accidents preceded the airport's closing c. 1972.

Sigmund Eisner began the manufacture of clothes in Red Bank c. 1886 in small, rented quarters. In 1903 he built his first Bridge Avenue factory to a design by Joseph Swannell, the four-story building with its end facing the street. By that time his uniform manufacturing business was growing rapidly. The extension at the left was built in 1905. A serious fire destroyed much of the plant in 1906. The fourth story of the original building was added at the time of rebuilding. This postcard probably dates from c. 1907.

Looking south on Bridge Avenue, from the Eisner factory, right of the trees. Notice the old-style railroad crossing which made escaping difficult if one was caught behind a downed gate.

The Eisner facilities expanded on both sides of Bridge Avenue and beyond. This postcard post-dates the 1917 construction of the large three-story building in the center right. Some buildings have since been demolished, such as the two-story building in the rear, but most of the plant on the west side of Bridge Avenue has been converted to the Galleria shops.

An interior of an Eisner sewing room from the early 1950s. Although this scene is well past their peak activity, the room suggests the capacity of a firm that fulfilled enormous uniform contracts at time of war and other periods of peak demand. (The Dorn's Collection.)

Modern education in Red Bank began with the 1871 construction of the Mechanic Street School. A college-educated principal was hired and grading-by-ability, begun two years earlier, was improved. Considerable discussion among the then modestly-educated populace preceded the erection of the costly, $10,000 brick, four-room school. Enrollment expanded and major expansions for classrooms and an auditorium were made. The school building, located west of Washington Street, was remodeled for offices in 1985.

A rapid rise in enrollment soon necessitated the erection of a second school. The four-room Oakland Street School, located between West and Pearl Streets, was built in 1877 and later expanded. It was remodeled as a restaurant and remains so today, following changes of operators. This view is from a *c.* 1910 postcard.

In 1895, youthful architect Fred Truex, who had graduated from the Red Bank High School only four years earlier, designed the new school for Red Bank's west side. The Shrewsbury Avenue School was erected on the southeast corner of Shrewsbury Avenue and Herbert Street. It was closed in 1924, a few years after the opening of the River Street School. This is an early-twentieth-century postcard view.

The River Street School, designed by Fred Truex in conjunction with Ernest Arend, was built in 1919, and expanded in 1926 and 1936. The school closed c. mid-1970s. The building has been proposed for historic register listing, its stature enhanced by retention of the original windows. Obtaining listing might provide an incentive for conversion to housing, which would result in the loss of the windows. Should preservation make more sense?

Richard Van Dyke Reid was displaced as principal when the Mechanic Street School was opened. At his death in 1915 he was described as "the last of the old-time schoolmasters of Monmouth." This is the school's picture of 1916. One can still have a stimulating discussion of the relative advantages of education then and now.

The Red Bank Catholic High School Class of 1913. Sister Mary Scholastica took charge of the St. James Convent in 1888 and served thirty-one years before being reassigned in 1919 to Star of the Sea Parish in Atlantic City. The picture was lent by Peg Jordan. Her mother, Alice Margaret Schmidt, proposed a 50th reunion celebration. Some classmates suggested otherwise, not willing to reveal their ages. Girls, you should have had the party, because it doesn't matter now.

Red Bank's first high school was built in 1901 on the east side of Branch Avenue following several years of local discussion. When a new three-story high school was built 1917–19 nearby on Harding Road, the above building was converted to a junior high school. Red Bank's high school system is now regionalized with Shrewsbury and Little Silver, with the school a 1975 structure in the latter town. The first high school was demolished in 1977. This is a postcard view from the early 1900s.

The Class of 1916 reflects noticeable change. Some students are even barely smiling. Was it faster film or a new posing practice? The picture is not annotated, nor is the June 14, 1916 *Register* much help. It did note that forty-five students will graduate, the largest number the system has produced. One would receive a gold prize worth $10 offered by Hamilton Price and read his winning essay on a subject relating to the growth and history of Red Bank.

William James "Count" Basie was born in Red Bank in 1904. Bill, as he was known locally, left town for Kansas City in 1934, joining the Bennie Moten Orchestra. Within a few years, he was its leader and the group was "discovered" and booked for Chicago and New York performances, beginning world-wide acclaim as jazz musicians. Basie retained an affinity for his home town and long-thought of himself as the title of one hit, "The Kid From Red Bank."

Joseph Oschwald's Carlton Theatre opened in November 1926 with a performance of *The Quarterback* with Richard Dix. It was designed by noted Newark theatre architect William E. Lehman and built by the construction company of the owner's son. Walter Reade was the lessee of the theatre, hailed as the paragon of beauty and convenience in its time. The Carlton was renamed in honor of Count Basie after his death in 1984.

Count Basie built a new home for his parents at their 229 Mechanic Street site in the eastern Red Bank Goosetown neighborhood. The Count's old piano was not going to be saved. Evelyn Leavens came upon the demolition scene and had Harvey Basie pose by the piano before it fell under the foundation site.

The new Harvey Basie house at 229 Mechanic Street. What musical history is buried here?

The Pilgrim Baptist Church built this edifice on the east side of Pearl Street, south of Front, in 1910. The congregation moved to Shrewsbury Avenue following their 1955 purchase of the Reformed Church's structure. The Pearl Street building is now the St Nicholas Russian Eastern Orthodox Church.

The first Grace Methodist Episcopal Church was moved to Shrewsbury and Leonard Streets in 1892 following the erection of their second edifice (see p. 36). A Dutch Reformed congregation was formed in 1902 and in time acquired the former M.E. church which they expanded and remodeled in 1915. They moved to Tinton Falls in 1956, building a new church. This one is now the Pilgrim Baptist Church. This view is from a c. 1910 postcard.

Sidney Conover was among Red Bank's wealthiest and best-known citizens. His financial success stemmed from his real estate acumen, while his familiarity came from his forty-year practice of riding around town on a wagon pulled by a pony. His small, swift steeds at times bested larger horses in Broad Street sleigh races. Conover often conducted business at the Globe Hotel. He died in 1913. (Collection of the Red Bank Public Library.)

An early-twentieth-century photograph of the Red Bank Orioles. They made news in 1924 when they sold their Newman Springs Road property and disbanded with a profit. Their land, purchased only three years prior, was allegedly becoming valuable. Presumably the property became the Red Bank Pirates stadium on the Tinton Falls side of that road, a site since developed as housing. (The Dorn's Collection.)

Robert Allen, one of Monmouth's most distinguished nineteenth-century lawyers, deserves to have his better side shown. However, the chance meeting with William Lufburrow in the early 1890s, captured from Andrew Coleman's second-story office, is charming. He wrote several acts for the New Jersey Legislature. One, which became known as "Robert Allen's law," was passed in 1852 and authorized a married woman to own property and collect rents outside her husband's control. He erected the building at the northwest corner of Front Street and Wharf Avenue when it was the center of the Red Bank business district. (Collection of the Red Bank Public Library.)

These firemen and their horse-drawn equipment left the Navesink Hook & Ladder Company firehouse on Mechanic Street to proceed south on Broad around 1885. If the picture seems familiar, perhaps you recall the cover of the Red Bank Fire Department's 100th anniversary booklet. (Collection of the Red Bank Public Library.)

The Navesink Hook & Ladder Company was organized in 1872. Their firehouse, built in 1880 after the disastrous New Year's fire, was located on the north side of Mechanic Street. Other serious fires, two in 1881 and a third in November 1882, convinced the town that adequate water supplies were a critical public need. Mechanic Street in the late nineteenth century was still lined with the smaller artisans' buildings that gave the street its name.

An elderly man and his youthful garden helpers walk east on Mechanic Street, perhaps in the 1880s. The background reflects the old character of the street as a home for artisans' shops. The Wild Building is on the southeast corner with Broad. The frame buildings would be replaced the early twentieth century. (Collection of the Red Bank Public Library.)

Charles R.D. Foxwell's superb photographs, notably street scenes, make this a better book. His photographic postcards are highly prized by collectors. Foxwell organized Red Bank's first photography club and opened a photo supply and stationery store. He was a justice of the peace for twenty-seven years until his death in 1944. He is shown here in his fireman's uniform in a c. 1900 photograph from the Collection of the Red Bank Public Library

Photographer Charles Foxwell was a member of Relief Engine Company #1. They are gathered here for an event, probably at their pre-1914 Pearl Street location.

Andrew R. Coleman, seen in the field, where he made a specialty of nature work. Coleman opened a gallery at Broad and Front Streets in 1892. He moved to the *Register* Building in 1912, becoming a staff photographer. His 1895 ad is a model of brevity and clarity, although not understatement: "My work is of the best and my prices are moderate. My out-door work is especially good." The picture is perhaps *c.* 1910. (The Dorn's Collection.)

Relief Engine Company #1, Red Bank's second fire company, was organized February 3, 1880, a month after the Naftal fire. After quarters at the R.R. Mount Building on West Front Street and a building on Pearl Street near Monmouth, a brick firehouse was erected on Drummond Place behind the town hall. This picture may date not long thereafter, with the town's equipment assembled for an event. (Collection of the Red Bank Public Library.)

Abram I. Elkus bought in 1906 a nearly finished house started for Henry J. Randall. The architect of this fine Colonial Revival is unknown. The Presbyterians bought the property from Judge Elkus' widow in 1949, planning a new church, with the Elkus residence attached as an education building. The house was later demolished.

Abram I. Elkus was born 1867 in New York City, studied law at Columbia, and began his distinguished practice in 1888. His legal work included service as a special United States attorney prosecuting fraud in bankruptcy proceedings. He served on the New York Court of Appeals. Elkus was ambassador to Turkey during the second Wilson administration, including the diplomatically difficult period prior to the United States entry in World War I. He was active in relief activities overseas. He died at his Tower Hill home in 1947. Red Bank Mayor Katharine Elkus White was his daughter.

Katharine Elkus White served Red Bank as mayor for three terms during 1951–56, and the nation as ambassador to Denmark for four years beginning in 1964. Diplomatic and political interests were stimulated at home. She lived in Constantinople, Turkey, where her father was ambassador, from 1916 to 1919 and attended the 1928 Democratic National Convention with her mother Gertrude, an alternate delegate. Mrs. White had a lengthy public service record, which included the distinction of being the first woman in the United States to head a toll road body, the New Jersey Highway Authority. She is pictured here *c.* 1953 gesturing to an acquaintance outside the borough hall.

T. THOMAS FORTUNE.

"The most noted man in Afro-American journalism is Thomas Fortune of New York," wrote I. Garland Penn in his 1891 *The Afro-American Press and Its Editors*, the source of this portrait. Fortune was born in 1856 in Florida. He began his journalism career there and came to own and edit *The New York Age*. His parents were slaves, and Fortune was a strong advocate for justice; his writings prompted Penn to note that "he never writes unless he makes somebody wince."

This Second Empire house at 94 West Bergen Place was built by shoe merchant John R. Bergen, likely in the late 1870s when the street was outside the limits of the newly organized town. Its listing on the National Register of Historic Places is owed to its association with T. Thomas Fortune, who owned it around the first decade of this century. Due to Fortune's stature in the national black community, many notable African-Americans visited him at Red Bank during his ownership.

Rector Place is a long block running north from West Front Street to Bridge Avenue. The Reverend William Dunnell built the three-story brick house on the west, or river side, at the curve in the road c. 1860s and inspired its name. This view is from a c. 1905 postcard.

South Street was cut through the White estate, running south from Branch Avenue to Pinckney Road. It contains one of Red Bank's oldest houses, the White homestead. The street was built up with housing in the late nineteenth and early twentieth centuries. This is a c. 1920 postcard view.

An early 1950s view of an Esso station formerly at the busy juncture of Riverside and Bridge Avenues with Highway 35. (The Dorn's Collection.)

The Mount-English Ford service enclosure was a classic c. 1930s streamlined-style commercial building. (The Dorn's Collection.)

Theodore Sickles was born in Shrewsbury and began a carriage-building business there. He came to Red Bank in 1876 and opened a Broad Street grocery business with John Trafford. Asher Parker was the second of three partners. The identity of the building is not clear, but it is known that the firm had an L-shaped lot backing into Mechanic Street. This is a c. 1890s photograph. (The Dorn's Collection.)

The casual viewer may not imagine that the office at 10 West Bergen Place was earlier a beer distribution warehouse, as shown in this late 1940s photograph. The building was erected as a plant for the Seaboard Ice Co. You are an aging baseball fan if you remember when a Ballantine blast was a Yankee home run. (The Dorn's Collection.)

This photograph is labeled "Mr. Mount" and attributing an identification without other information can be risky as quite a few Mounts populated the area since George Mount arrived in Monmouth County *c.* 1669. One expects he is John W. Mount, even without trying to match his bicycle with either of those below. He founded a carriage-building business in Red Bank in 1860. (Collection of the Red Bank Public Library.)

Mount's carriage-building and harness business grew steadily, and by the time of this 1880s photograph, was housed in a substantial building at the northeast corner of Maple Avenue and White Streets. John H. Mount, son of the founder, guided its entry into the motor age *c.* 1905 when the firm began to build auto bodies and sell automobiles. (The Dorn's Collection.)

A fire on the night of June 12, 1908, destroyed the John W. Mount Co. carriage and automobile plant at the northeast corner of Maple and White Streets. The blaze began in a second-story paint shop and quickly consumed the plant with its highly combustible contents and floors saturated with paint and oil. Nearby houses were threatened, with one next door burned. About 100 carriages under construction were lost.

Lower Maple Avenue became Red Bank's first automobile strip by the 1920s, a district that later relocated to Shrewsbury Avenue beyond the borough's border. This June 11, 1928 view from south of Maple's corner with Gold Street shows at the right Homer Methot's new showroom for Jordan automobiles. The four-story building was the Mount-English Ford showroom at the northwest corner with Monmouth Street, while Ed von Kattengell's place on the southeast corner is obscured.

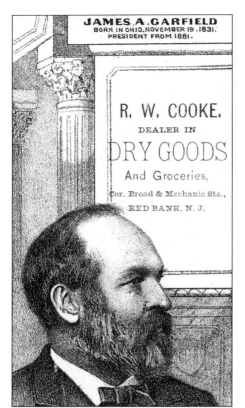

Merchant R.W. Cooke advertised his store with a series of presidential trade cards in 1881. The year can be inferred from the terms of office. The others indicated their subjects' full terms, while Garfield both took office and died in 1881. His close association with the shore stems from his death in Long Branch on September 19, 1881. He had been sent there for the salubrious qualities of the oceanfront environs after being shot on July 2, 1881.

The Caramel Ice Cream Shop (we'll spell it the simple way, thank you), on Riverside Avenue, just east of Bridge Avenue, has the character of a highway eatery, c. 1951. Later remodelings built a restaurant around this simple shell.

The Pleasant Inn's varied career included a spell as prohibition speak-easy. Its construction followed an often-repeated local form, building a business extension outside a house. This postcard is likely c. 1930. The locale was the northwest corner of Shrewsbury Avenue and Newman Springs Road, a site now occupied by a gas station.

Charles Duppler, a veteran of the Franco-Prussian War, founded the Mecca Inn in 1905. Formerly a chef in New York hotels, he came to the county to improve his health, as former New Yorkers still do today. His inn, located at the northeast corner of Shrewsbury Avenue and Newman Springs Road, had three large dining rooms, a bar, and seventeen sleeping rooms. This view is from a c. 1915 postcard

Streets, before paving, were liable to be either dusty or muddy. The street sprinkler was essential for controlling dust. This turn-of-the-century example is seen on Washington Street.

Harry Crossley built this fine Colonial Revival house on the northeast corner of Maple Avenue and Le Roy Place, c. 1905. The architect is unknown. The building is now occupied by Catholic Charities and bears resemblance to this c. 1915 postcard. However, the original wood shingles, in lieu of the present vinyl siding, enhanced its character, a reminder of the considerable use of that material on the shore in the two prior decades.

The Colombia Poultry Farm had a large duck-raising operation, owned by Frank R. Burr in 1890, located on Branch Avenue. About five hundred ducks were separated into breeding and market flocks. Burr had experimented for five years before perfecting his artificial incubation methods. Frank H. Hodges owned it in the early 1900s, broadening the brood to include several breeds of chickens. (The Dorn's Collection.)

White Street was described in the 1931 Red Bank Plan as neither a traffic street nor a business street because of its narrow width. This late 1940s view looks east toward its bottleneck at Broad Street. White Street found a new calling: a parking street. (The Dorn's Collection.)

N<u>o</u>   33

CHANCE ON AN
AUSTIN ROADSTER
to be given away by
Sally Ann Lee, Hairdresser
105 Monmouth St., Red Bank, N. J.
TICKETS, $1.00

All those having a Permanent Wave before June 15th will receive One chance FREE. The drawing will be held at the Publix Carlton Theatre, Red Bank, N. J., Mondny, June 15th, at 9 P. M.

Russell Tetley's first reaction to the call on June 15, 1931, telling him he had won a car was to ignore the imagined prankster. Subsequent telephone calls from friends did not convince him. Finally a visit from a policeman requesting that he remove the car from the Carlton's stage as they were eager to begin the next show made Russell realize it was no prank.

Although Russell Tetley cut a sporting figure in his new Austin, when he and Grace Rudy married in 1933, the car, their third, became expendable. They answered a local ad by a Polish man seeking to send a car to his wife in Poland. He bought it and it arrived there safely, as Grace's picture of the buyer's wife in the car attests.

The library's label identifies this as the 1891 Thanksgiving football game between east and west Red Bank. The players are identified, although their team is not. From left to right are: (front row) John Forsythe, Joe Blaisdell, Tom Rose, Joe Green, Bob Hance, and Haddon Ivins; (back row) George Cooper, Steve Tallman, Bob Forsythe, Frank Morris, and in the extreme rear, perhaps the fullback, Al Cooper. (Collection of the Red Bank Public Library.)

William H. Reid, born a free man in Virginia in 1840, had the unusual distinction of serving in both the Confederate and Union armies during the Civil War. Early in the war, he served under General Longstreet in the Black Horse Cavalry. Moving north after realizing the unjustness of the south's cause, Reid enlisted in New York's 26th Regiment. He lived in a house he owned on Mechanic Street for over sixty years. Reid made his casket in 1913 and dug a brick-lined grave in Eatontown's White Ridge Cemetery, where he was laid to rest in 1927. (Collection of the Red Bank Public Library.)

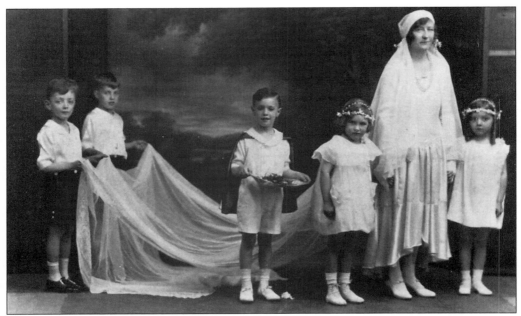

A group of five pleased children and a seemingly apprehensive adult participate in a *c.* late 1920s May crowning ceremony at St. James. Lois Pennington, the sweet young girl at the right, grew up to have a sweet young girl of her own, Catherine Ann Jacoby, the lender of this photograph.

Charles Hammer and his goat cart photographed in front of a backdrop. He lived in East Side Park, considered a suburb of Red Bank in the early century, but it is actually in Fair Haven. How did they get in this book? The author likes goats. As Gabrielan was heard to say, "Putting this book together was hard work. I needed a little fun. That's all folks (until Volume 2)."